Guns, Germs, and Steel

BARNES & NOBLE® READER'S COMPANION™
Today's take on tomorrow's classics.

FICTION
THE CORRECTIONS by Jonathan Franzen
I KNOW WHY THE CAGED BIRD SINGS by Maya Angelou
THE JOY LUCK CLUB by Amy Tan
THE LOVELY BONES by Alice Sebold
THE POISONWOOD BIBLE by Barbara Kingsolver
THE RED TENT by Anita Diamant
WE WERE THE MULVANEYS by Joyce Carol Oates
WHITE TEETH by Zadie Smith

NONFICTION
THE ART OF WAR by Sun Tzu
A BRIEF HISTORY OF TIME by Stephen Hawking
GUNS, GERMS, AND STEEL by Jared Diamond
JOHN ADAMS by David McCullough

BARNES & NOBLE® READER'S COMPANION™

JARED DIAMOND'S

Guns, Germs, and Steel

BARNES
& NOBLE
B O O K S

EDITORIAL DIRECTOR Justin Kestler
EXECUTIVE EDITOR Ben Florman
DIRECTOR OF TECHNOLOGY Tammy Hepps

SERIES EDITOR John Crowther
MANAGING EDITOR Vincent Janoski

WRITER Anne Williams
EDITOR Matt Blanchard
DESIGN Dan O. Williams, Matt Daniels

This edition published by Spark Publishing

Spark Publishing
A Division of SparkNotes LLC
120 Fifth Avenue, 8th Floor
New York, NY 10011

ISBN 1-58663-863-7

Library of Congress Cataloging-in-Publication Data available upon request

Printed and bound in the United States

Contents

BARNES & NOBLE® READER'S COMPANION™

WITH INTELLIGENT CONVERSATION AND ENGAGING
commentary from a variety of perspectives, BARNES
& NOBLE READER'S COMPANIONS are the perfect
complement to today's most widely read and
discussed books.

Whether you're reading on your own or as part of a
book club, BARNES & NOBLE READER'S COMPANIONS
provide insights and perspectives on today's most
interesting reads: What are other people saying about
this book? What's the author trying to tell me?

○ ○ ○

Pick up the BARNES & NOBLE READER'S COMPANION
to learn more about what you're reading. From the
big picture down to the details, you'll get today's take
on tomorrow's classics.

Guns, Germs, and Steel

From Apes to Atom Bombs

Guns, Germs, and Steel takes on a grand task: explaining the vast complexity of human history in a single stroke.

○ ○ ○

EVEN THE MOST CASUAL OBSERVER of human history probably wonders why it is that western Europeans conquered vast native populations on other continents instead of the other way around. Why are Spanish and Portuguese spoken all over South America today but no Aztec and Inca languages spoken in Spain and Portugal? Why were white Europeans never taken as slaves by invading groups of black Africans? More generally, what particular sets of circumstances account for the different paths and paces of human history in the various regions of the world? These critical and eternal questions form the center of Jared Diamond's *Guns, Germs, and Steel,* an ambitious and compelling account of humanity's last 13,000 years.

Of course, it's the victors who explain (and justify) human history. So these big questions—if they're considered at all—are typically answered in terms of the natural superiority of the conquerors. A number of explanations of human history make presumptions about racial, cultural, and intellectual inequalities: "White Europeans were more intelligent"; "The conquered natives were savages"; and so on. But such explanations are simplistic and incorrect. Even if they could be true (and Diamond's opposition to racial arguments is clear at the outset), they still can't explain how these alleged inequalities arose in the first place. Diamond sets out to determine the *ultimate* causes of racial and cultural differences in the earliest eras of human history. He tries to find the points at which groups of people diverged for the first time and why. He seeks the answers in purely scientific, culturally neutral terms. In the end, he finds that racial explanations fail to hold up under this type of scrutiny.

Throughout *Guns, Germs, and Steel,* Diamond focuses on the environments in which various human cultures developed. In his view, the environment—specifically, the plants and animals native to a region—have done the most to determine the fates of the different groups of people throughout world history. In areas that lacked domesticable plants and animals, farming (and the sedentary lifestyle farming allowed) couldn't develop, so people remained largely in primitive hunter-gathering tribes. Where these resources *were* available, cultures progressed toward the development of towns, cities, language, and technology—and eventually the exploration and conquering of other lands.

It's not quite that simple, though. Diamond believes that many complex factors were involved, and he goes to great lengths to examine them all. But ultimately he returns to his conclusion that environmental factors have been the greatest determinants of the fates of human societies. In his own one-sentence summary of the book, Diamond states, "History followed different courses for different peoples because of differences among people's environments, not because of biological differences among peoples themselves."

What sets *Guns, Germs, and Steel* apart is the number of different scientific and academic disciplines it draws on. Diamond isn't a historian but a scientist, trained in molecular physiology, evolutionary biology, and biogeography. He expertly ties together recent discoveries in numerous other scientific disciplines, including genetics, behavioral ecology, molecular biology, epidemiology, biochemistry, linguistics, archaeology, and the histories of technology, written language, and political organization. The result is a work both broad and deep, covering virtually all aspects of human development, in all areas of the world, from prehistory through the modern era. To answer such enormous questions and to synthesize so much scientific theory into a work that somehow remains eminently readable is an awesomely impressive feat in itself.

PROLOGUE
YALI'S QUESTION

Diamond sets us out on our journey by introducing the central question he seeks to answer in *Guns, Germs, and Steel*. In 1972, when Diamond was studying bird evolution in New Guinea, a local politician named Yali asked him a question: "Why is it that you white people developed so much cargo and brought it to New Guinea, but we black people had little cargo of our own?" By cargo, Yali meant tools, technology, material goods, and so on—the trappings of modern civilization. This simple question of how wealth and power came to be distributed over time stayed with Diamond for years, eventually inspiring him to answer it with *Guns, Germs, and Steel*.

A work with such enormous and far-reaching arguments is always hard to organize, but Diamond's prologue does a great deal to simplify the journey for us. He lays out the order of issues he plans to tackle and the reasons behind his slightly circuitous discussion. His methodology, as he explains, is to describe concrete historical episodes and their proximate— or nearest—causes, then to push back from them to the larger, more abstract ultimate causes. Using that framework, he hopes to ground the complex scientific material he covers in a more accessible historical context.

PART ONE
FROM EDEN TO CAJAMARCA

Diamond begins by tracing human evolution from our earliest divergence from our ape ancestors until the end of the last Ice Age, 13,000 years ago. Along the way, he provides an overview of how humans spread from Africa to other continents.

After five or six million years of evolution in Africa, the first human ancestors to spread to Eurasia were *Homo erectus*—the famous "Java man" skeleton. Fossil evidence of *Homo sapiens* indicate they were present by about half a million years ago in Africa and Eurasia, evolving over time into Neanderthals, with their crude tools and artifacts. Then about 50,000 years ago, human history took off at a rapid pace with the emergence of the Cro-Magnon, in what Diamond terms the "Great Leap

Forward." This leap marks the first time humans spread to other continents since the initial movement from Africa to Eurasia.

Humans colonized the different continents at different times, often corresponding to times when the existence of glaciers made travel across bodies of water possible. Australia and New Guinea were occupied roughly 40,000 years ago, followed by the Americas sometime between 14,000 and 35,000 years ago. The dates of the arrival of humans in both of these regions coincide with the extinction of the continent's largest prehistoric mammals—a coincidence Diamond attributes to newly arrived humans overhunting large species that previously had no natural enemies.

By the close of the last Ice Age—about 11000 B.C.—humans had populated all of the world's major continents. Although some areas, like Africa, had supported human populations for a longer time, some more recently colonized areas, like North America, saw faster population growth and development. But across all continents, genetically modern humans were engaged in a similar hunter-gatherer lifestyle. In 11000 B.C. it would've been impossible to predict where "civilization" would develop most rapidly. The playing field seemed essentially even.

> Similar early humans **encountered** vastly different environments in the **areas** they inhabited—and this **must have** influenced their **development.**

But despite the level playing field, similar early humans encountered vastly different environments in the areas they inhabited—and this must have influenced their development. To test this theory, Diamond compares the small-scale colonization of Polynesia with the large-scale colonization of the major continents.

✈ Between about 1200 B.C. and 500 A.D., descendants of people from an area north of New Guinea had colonized nearly all of the thousands of islands of Polynesia. These settlers all came from the same population group but encountered environments that differed radically from island to island. Over time, these environmental differences manifested themselves in societal differences as well. Despite coming from identical genetic stock, these Polynesian peoples developed enormous differences in behavior, population densities, and social customs within just a few generations. Where agriculture was possible, populations became denser, societies more stratified, and power struggles more likely. In areas that supported only nomadic hunting and gathering, dispersed tribes lived peacefully in small groups.

Diamond offers a dramatic example of the human differences environment can create, using the example of an 1835 clash between the farmers and hunter-gatherers on the Chatham Islands off New Zealand. In that year, fewer than a thousand Maori people arrived by ship from New Zealand and destroyed the native Moriori population in a matter of days, killing everyone in sight. The Maori came from a densely populated and technologically sophisticated farming culture with strong centralized leadership and a history of war. The Moriori, on the other hand, were a loosely organized population of isolated hunter-gatherers with a culture of peace and compromise. Of course, the Maori crushed the Moriori.

But the Maori and the Moriori were *exactly the same people*, separated only by the different environments they had lived in for the past few generations. The Maori were descendants of Polynesian farmers who arrived in New Zealand in 1000 A.D. Some Maori went on to the Chatham Islands soon after—these groups became the Moriori. Encountering favorable conditions in New Zealand, the Maori intensified their farming. The Moriori, meanwhile, reverted to a hunter-gatherer lifestyle because their new land couldn't support farming. Within only a few centuries, then, the very same people evolved into radically different cultures based on their environments. It's a small-scale example but a compelling one.

The 1532 encounter between the Inca emperor Atahuallpa and the Spanish explorer Francisco Pizarro—the "Collision at Cajamarca" described in Chapter 3—provides another example of a small army of invaders destroying a much larger group in a very short time. In this clash, an army of 168 Spaniards killed thousands of the approximately 80,000 assembled Inca soldiers, caused the rest to flee, and took their emperor hostage in a single day. But this wasn't a clash between farmers and hunter-gatherers. After all, the Inca empire was vast, agriculturally sophisticated, and extremely well organized.

But the Spaniards succeeded in this and many subsequent encounters with native people because of a number of specific factors. First, they brought guns, powerful steel weapons, and armor, while the Indians had only clubs and hand axes. Second, the Spaniards rode on horses, which not only allowed them speed and protection from Indian ground troops, but were also completely foreign to the New World and frightening to the Indians. Third, the Spaniards arrived at Cajamarca after a smallpox epidemic had swept through South America, courtesy of Spanish settlers who had arrived a decade earlier. The epidemic had killed the previous Inca emperor and sparked a civil war over his succession, leaving a less unified empire. Fourth, Europe's technology, paired with political organization, created the ships and sponsors that made exploration possible. Finally, the Spaniards had written language while the Inca empire did not. The Spanish were able to learn beforehand everything that was known about the New World. Having read detailed written accounts, they could model their attack on previous successful approaches. Atahuallpa and his men could learn about the Spaniards only through word of mouth, so they knew nothing of Spain's previous conquests in Central America.

These factors—guns and steel, domesticated animals, nasty germs, shipbuilding technology, and written language—are the proximate causes for European dominance over the New World. Taken together, they explain why the clashes turned out as they did. But they still don't explain why Europe had these things and conquered natives didn't. To figure that out, Diamond pushes back further still, hoping to find the reasons behind the reasons.

PART TWO
THE RISE AND SPREAD
OF FOOD PRODUCTION

The search for ultimate causes all starts with food. For Diamond, food production is the single most important determinant of a society's development. Where we find domesticable plants and animals, we also find societies that developed the package of advantages—the "guns, germs, and steel"—that allowed for one culture's dominance over another. Farming and herding yield far more food per square acre than hunting and gathering, and this increase in calories produced can support a higher population density. Also, because farmers settle and live near their crops, they can support a higher birthrate compared to nomadic people, who can't have more babies than they can easily carry.

Sheer numbers, then, account for much of the advantage farmers ultimately have over hunter-gatherers. But there are other factors too. Farmers can create and put aside food surpluses, which allows for specialization within a society. Because only some of the members of a farming society need to be involved in food production, others are free to become inventors who develop new technologies, scribes who preserve information, or conquering soldiers who defend and attack. If the land doesn't support any plants suitable for farming, these advantages are ultimately missing.

Food production began independently in only a few places in the world and then spread to others. Carbon dating and other scientific clues suggest there are only five areas where food production definitely began: the Fertile Crescent (parts of modern-day Israel, Turkey, Syria, and Iraq), China, Mesoamerica, the Andes mountains of South America, and the eastern United States. A few additional areas are still under debate. In virtually all other parts of the world, food production began later, at widely different times and through different means. Diamond makes the start of farming, and its spread from limited origins to eventual adoption throughout the world, his focus throughout the rest of Part Two.

First, how did people begin to farm? Hunter-gatherers didn't just wake up one morning to see crops growing outside their camps. The shift from hunting and gathering to farming and herding happened gradually, in piecemeal fashion. It was the result of a continuing set of decisions made by early peoples.

Because early man's primary goal was survival, the question of how to use one's time was critical. Activities were only justifiable if they made survival more possible. Where farming might yield a greater concentration of calories and protein, it would be worth the time and effort. But if game and wild foods were more plentiful, hunting and gathering could win out. The two lifestyles were more blended than we think of today: many farmers supplemented their crops with wild plants and animals, and many hunter-gatherers planted some amount of crops to return to after foraging for months. Once farming techniques were developed, people in neighboring areas could see them in action and adopt them in whole or in part. Diamond describes the two methods beginning as "alternative strategies competing with each other." As we learn, the farmers most often won the competition, but the transition wasn't immediate.

Several big factors governed the human decision to gradually adopt farming over hunting and gathering. First was the decline in wild food resources, especially large game animals, which became less abundant or even extinct over time. At the same time, changes in climate (among other factors) made domesticable wild plants more abundant. Technological developments led to tools that made it easier and more efficient to collect wild plants, especially cereals. Baskets, blades, and mortars and pestles, originally developed in the Fertile Crescent after 11000 B.C. for use with wild grains, made farming possible as well.

Farming societies tended to have larger, denser populations, which made it more likely that farmers would displace hunter-gatherers in the areas where they overlapped. But these larger populations also forced

> *"Our failure to domesticate even a single major new food plant in modern times suggests that ancient peoples really may have domesticated all the ones worth domesticating."*

farming societies to develop better techniques, cultivate more land, and produce more food. More food would generate greater population growth, which would require more food, and so on in a cycle.

Although early farmers encountered thousands of species of plants, it turns out that only a few were suitable for domestication. Diamond's discussion of the science and genetics of plants is detailed and fascinating. One of the most interesting points he makes is that the latrine may have been the greatest "lab" available to early farmers, offering accidental discoveries as the seeds and berries hunter-gatherers ate subsequently germinated and grew from their feces. This "artificial selection" by humans would help to create more productive plants, as humans would chose the biggest and best seeds and fruits to eat in the first place.

In many cases, domestication was possible because of specific genetic mutations in plants. In the Fertile Crescent, for example, certain naturally occurring wheat plants carried a mutation that prevented their stalks from shattering and spreading their seeds on the ground. This characteristic would be disastrous in the wild because the plant would never reproduce —but it was ideal for humans, who could harvest the stalks and remove the seeds themselves. These mutant seeds would then be the ones "planted" at latrine sites and ultimately cultivated. It was these types of genetic accidents that led to the domestication of many crops and helped the transformation of many wild species into the cultivated foods we know today.

Some locations for early plant domestication are obvious, but there were other suitable climates 10,000 years ago where agriculture never got started. The suitable conditions of the places like the Fertile Crescent— the "cradle of civilization"—are well known and well documented. But highly fertile soils in California, Europe, and Australia are among the most productive farmland today, so why didn't agriculture develop there? Was it a lack of plants or a lack of initiative among local people? Diamond argues that although these fertile areas were suitable for farming and contained many native plants, they lacked the *right* plants. In fact, the specific plants we associate with these modern-day farming areas were all introduced from elsewhere. Local populations often readily adopted these plants once they were introduced, so we can dismiss the argument that the local people were unmotivated or lacked the ability to recognize the value of farming.

But the odds against early humans developing organized agriculture were high in some respects. Only a few thousand of the world's 200,000 wild plants are edible, and only a few hundred of these have been domesticated. Of these, only twelve are good enough sources of nutrients and calories to account for eighty percent of the world's agriculture— and these twelve powerhouse crops were domesticated thousands of years ago. Even with advanced technology, we haven't domesticated any major new food crops in modern times. With these limitations, it's easier to imagine an area with only one or two suitable native plants where farming didn't begin spontaneously.

And even one or two suitable plants in a region was no guarantee that agriculture would develop. As Diamond's holistic view suggests, the determining factor isn't a single plant but the total package of plants—

combined with suitable climate, geography, and other natural resources. Hunter-gatherers couldn't change their lifestyles for a single crop. They needed a whole package of crops that would provide most, if not all, of their dietary needs before they could settle down to farming. Only a very few locations—the Fertile Crescent being the most notable—offered that package.

Then came the animals. The domestication of large animals contributed enormously to the successful transition to farming. Animals also provided valuable protein-rich food, warm clothing, and materials for building. They could pull plows, allowing farmers to cultivate larger areas. Their manure was a valuable fertilizer, enabling cultivated land to produce more food per acre. The existence of beasts of burden may have hastened the development of key technologies too. It's no surprise that wagons and carts first emerged in areas where there were animals to pull them. And in times of conflict, soldiers on horseback had an obvious advantage over foot soldiers.

Even more significant was the collection of deadly germs that evolved from domesticated animals. Many of the first domesticators of animals became sick and died. But over time, people living in close proximity with animals evolved immunities to diseases, like smallpox, that originated in animals. Much of the domination of farmers over hunter-gatherers was the result of accidental infection, as immune farmers entered an area and breathed their germs on the natives.

As with plants, the availability of domesticable animals in a region played a part in determining the fate of its people, but it doesn't explain everything. Wild animals, just like wild plants, needed certain key traits to make them suitable, and only a few of these animals met the criteria. In examining which animals could be domesticated and why, Diamond offers what he calls the "*Anna Karenina* principle." Mirroring the famous first line of Tolstoy's novel—"Happy families are all alike; every unhappy family is unhappy in its own way"—Diamond makes the conclusion, "Domesticable animals are all alike; every undomesticable animal is undomesticable in its own way." While there's no single characteristic that guarantees success, there are many points for failure.

To be domesticated, an animal must meet many criteria. It must be large enough to be useful. It must be able to survive on a vegetable diet that farmers can grow or gather for it. While meat-eating mammals might be a good food source for humans, they would require farmers to supply a meat diet, which would in turn require the farmers to grow food to feed the animal's food—an impractical cycle. A domesticable animal also needs to grow fast enough to mature within a reasonable time frame. It must be willing to breed in captivity. Lastly, it must have a friendly and calm enough disposition to allow humans near it (this eliminates the grizzly bear, which meets all the other criteria). Generally, the best candidates are animals that can live well in groups and have a specific social structure to their herds. As it turns out, only a few animals possess all of the necessary qualities. Of the 148 large herbivorous mammals, only fourteen have ever been successfully domesticated. Most of these were originally found in Eurasia.

Just like crops, once domesticated animals were introduced to an area, native people adopted them easily. This easy adaptation suggests that native peoples everywhere would've domesticated suitable candidates if they had had any of their own. A classic example is the case of the Native Americans. Though we often think of the image of a Plains Indian on horseback, it's easy to forget that horses aren't native to the New World— they originally came from Eurasia. Many Native American tribes, after seeing the obvious advantages horses offered, began capturing them from the Europeans and using them for their own purposes.

Diamond's last big idea in his discussion of the origin of farming is one of his most compelling and simple theories. In Chapter 10, "Spacious Skies and Tilted Axes," Diamond argues that the orientations of the largest continents determined not just their suitability for farming but also the likelihood that farming techniques would spread. Although just a handful of areas developed farming independently, many more areas— especially in Eurasia—adopted it even in prehistoric times. Yet on other continents, farming never spread to certain suitable areas even when agricultural societies existed nearby.

For example, crops spread early and quickly from their origins in the Fertile Crescent to Europe—but they never made the move from the Mexican highlands to South America. In part, Diamond traces this difference to the axes of the continents. While Eurasia's orientation is east-west, the Americas run north-south. Farming techniques could spread easily along an east-west axis because most of that axis would be at roughly the same latitude—hence, the entire axis would have a similar climate and rainfall. Spreading farming techniques on a north-south axis, on the other hand, was difficult. Even along short distances, latitude differences cause significant climatic changes, different lengths of days, and so on. In short, different latitudes were rarely able to support the same crops. Even when two regions had compatible climates, there were often barriers between the two regions, areas in which their crops *couldn't* grow. For example, the Mexican highlands and the South American Andes shared similar climate conditions and could've supported the same crops—if only the hot lowlands of Central America didn't come between them.

PART THREE
FROM FOOD TO
GUNS, GERMS, AND STEEL

Diamond now turns our attention to the next step, moving from the development of farming (the ultimate cause) to the development of the "guns, germs, and steel" (the proximate causes) that determined history's winners.

Now that we've established when, where, and how farming developed and spread (or failed to spread), we look at what arose next—how the sedentary lifestyle created by farming gave rise to disease, language, technology, and centralized government. In four short chapters, Diamond provides a comprehensive, though whirlwind, tour of the development of these major aspects of human society. Each of these chapters could easily be a book in itself. One of Diamond's great accomplishments is that he not only distills huge concepts and explains vast connections, but does so in a manner that gives us the confidence to understand a complicated topic and the curiosity to learn more about it.

We begin with the history of disease, a subject Diamond is especially qualified to discuss. The science is dense but approachable. He describes in detail the development of major diseases from early animal hosts to the crowd-borne epidemics we've known throughout history. As Diamond explains, nearly all of the major epidemic diseases humans have faced—smallpox, malaria, measles, and so on—have evolved from animal pathogens. We can even trace the current AIDS epidemic back to a virus found in wild monkeys. Many of the biggest killers evolved from cattle and pigs—animals that lived in groups and spread disease throughout their herds. Humans who lived in close proximity to these animals (mainly the sedentary farmer-herders of Eurasia) fell victim to these mutated animal germs. While a stricken farmer certainly wouldn't have deemed these diseases another Eurasian advantage, they would ultimately contribute more to the success of Eurasian conquerors than any other factor.

To develop and spread, epidemic diseases needed high human population densities. The symptoms of epidemic diseases—coughing, open sores, diarrhea, and so on—are generally methods for germs to travel from one host to another, so the crowding that came with the rise of farm-fed cities made epidemics possible. Though everyone in an area might get sick, not everyone would die. Survivors would be immune and would often pass on their immunity to their children. Over time, more immunity developed as natural selection favored genes that protected humans from disease. As a result, farming societies could eventually live among animal-borne diseases without being destroyed.

But these Eurasian diseases came as a complete surprise for the populations of the New World. Although natives of the New World often lived

"All other things being equal, technology develops fastest in large productive regions with large human populations, many potential inventors, and many competing societies."

as farmers in dense population groups just like their Eurasian counterparts, they did not have the same types of domesticated animals as Eurasians and thus didn't develop the same immunities to animal-borne diseases. While guns and steel were certainly factors in Europe's conquest of the Americas, the germs the Europeans accidentally brought along with them were often the deciding factor. In many cases, disease wiped out entire tribes in a short time.

Farming and the population density it brought were critical factors in *all* the major advantages history's winners enjoyed—not just germs but also technology and the development and spread of written language.

Writing, like agriculture, developed independently in only a few places: the Fertile Crescent, southern Mexico, China, and Egypt. (Though there is some doubt about whether the development of writing in China—and especially Egypt—was completely independent, or whether these populations had some knowledge of the writing systems initially developed in the Fertile Crescent.)

Not surprisingly, we see that the first areas to develop writing were those that had developed farming first as well. These highly developed agricultural societies had evolved over thousands of years to support specialized classes of scribes, who were fed on surplus food and devoted their time to developing writing systems. The need for bureaucracies to control and manage surplus food was often directly behind the development of systems of writing. Interestingly, most of the earliest written material uncovered by archaeologists involves topics such as taxation and royal accounts. Early writing wasn't intended for the masses but for an elite group who recorded assets and material for kings.

Writing systems spread quickly among neighboring cultures, especially along east-west trade routes in Eurasia. Diamond's description of the adoption of writing is an excellent case study for how technologies in general spread among peoples. Typically, writing spread when people in an area came into contact with a written system in a neighboring area and decided to create a system of their own for their unique spoken language. Rather than invent from scratch, they based their efforts on what they had encountered. In the case of "blueprint copying," groups would copy or modify an existing system or systems of writing, using the same symbols in new ways. Other human inventors developed written language through "idea diffusion," in which people had only a basic idea to work with: understanding that a written system *could* be created, they would build their own specific system from scratch.

In either case, a group first had to encounter an *existing* system for writing—and this was more likely to occur in Eurasia, where cultures that shared climate and geography were in regular contact. As with all technologies and innovations, the diffusion of writing along the north-south axes of the Americas and Africa was much slower.

A fascinating example of how written language was developed in early history comes from the story of a Cherokee man named Sequoyah, who around 1820 developed a complete set of symbols for writing the

Cherokee language after seeing how valuable such a written system was for white men. Knowing nothing of written English, he borrowed some letters, modified others, and invented some symbols from scratch. In the end, the tribe quickly adopted Sequoyah's entire writing system. With a nearly 100 percent literacy rate, the Cherokees went on to purchase printing presses, modify them to print their symbols, and publish books and newspapers in their language.

By now, we're familiar with Diamond's explanation for the development and spread of technologies: population densities led to sedentary, stratified societies with excess goods and classes of people who had time and impetus to invent and develop tools and ideas. And geographic and climatic boundaries influenced how likely it was that a given group would encounter a new technology created elsewhere. When they did, they would typically adopt it in one of two ways. They might see the value of it and begin to make and use it themselves. Or, if lacking it put them at a serious disadvantage (as was often the case with guns), they might be overwhelmed and taken over by the group that had the technology, with the survivors of the encounter ultimately merging with the advantaged group.

But Diamond has a challenge here, in that some cultures just *seem* less receptive than others to new inventions. Although history gives us countless examples of groups adopting useful new tools when they're exposed to them, it's also filled with stories of tribes who encountered modern technologies and rejected them—or adopted and later abandoned them.

What accounts for these differences? Here, Diamond skirts the issue a bit. He argues that because readiness to adopt new technology varied from society to society within the same geographic region and also varied within the same society at different points in history, it can be essentially factored out. He writes: "The myriad factors affecting innovativeness make the historian's task paradoxically easier, by converting societal variation in innovativeness into essentially a random variable. That means that, over a large enough area (such as a whole continent) at any particular time, some proportion of societies is likely to be innovative." With this

The name game

Diamond has referred to *Guns, Germs, and Steel* as a "Peterson's Field Guide to human societies." He also prefers the subtitle of the British edition of his book, "A Short History of Everybody for the Last 13,000 Years."

statement, Diamond dismisses the notion that certain types of people are inherently more innovative than others, claiming that all types are innovative at some points in history and aren't at others.

Diamond is much more effective when he analyzes the specific conditions that tend to make a culture more receptive to new technologies. In addition to the conditions he has described as common to mature, densely populated societies—which we're quite familiar with by now—he adds the idea that proximity to other societies and competition within and among societies also make societies more receptive to new technology.

In populous and fragmented Europe, for instance, innovations were constantly imported and exported from society to society. A society's failure to adopt a new technology, especially a weapon, could be fatal if that society's neighbors embraced it. In contrast, isolated, unified societies could easily abandon innovation, especially where powerful groups in the society opposed it. Such was the case with Japan's abandonment of guns. Guns reached Japan in 1543, and the Japanese were so impressed that they began manufacturing their own. By 1600, they had more than any other country. But within a relatively brief period, the Samurai elite had managed to end gun manufacturing and eliminate nearly every existing gun. Only in an isolated island environment could this abandonment occur without a neighboring society taking advantage.

When Diamond tackles the question of why Europe was the first to send explorers to the New World rather than Japan or China (where many critical technologies, including shipbuilding were invented), he concludes that perhaps it was Europe's multiple cultures in competition that made innovation more possible. Christopher Columbus asked many monarchs to support his trip before Ferdinand and Isabel of Spain said yes. A Chinese explorer, on the other hand, would've had only one royal family to ask.

Next, now that Diamond has firmly established the role of agriculture and the farming lifestyle in generating higher population densities, he moves on to examine the stages of human organization that accompany these growing densities. In Chapter 14, "From Egalitarianism to Kleptocracy," he traces the history of human associations from small bands and tribes to elaborate states, demonstrating how larger population densities required more complicated organizations.

The smallest unit of society is the band, with five to eighty people who are typically nomadic and usually related by blood or marriage. In this type of group, leadership is informal, there are no fixed structures for conflict resolution, and there is no specialization of function—everyone in the band is involved in the work of the band to find food and survive.

The next level of societal organization is the tribe, with hundreds of people in kin-based clans, living in fixed settlements. Government is egalitarian, with informal and often problematic conflict resolution systems. Specialization is limited, as most people are involved in food production. The history of New Guinea, for one, provides a prime example of this kind of tribal organization.

Next up the ladder are chiefdoms, which encompass thousands of people related through class and proximity, but not blood. Government and conflict resolution is centralized, and rule is often hereditary. Chiefdoms also typically feature intensive food production and some division of labor. Many examples of chiefdoms can be found throughout the history of Polynesia.

States, the largest unit of societal organization, contain more than 50,000 people in many villages and cities, related by class and residence. States have highly intensive food production, many levels of bureaucracy, formalized laws, a highly specialized division of labor, tax-based economies, and public works such as irrigation systems.

But how did the transition from kin-based tribal societies to large centralized ones occur? In some regions, rising population densities simply made it necessary to assign different functions to different parts of society, with some people in charge of running things, particularly the transfer of surplus goods. But more often than not, the transition of a people from one type of organization to another was the result of wars of conquest, with the losing group merged into the winner. In some cases, small tribes joined together in advance of an outside threat (such as the Cherokee tribes in North America).

Population density plays a key role in all instances of the evolution of societal organization. Just as denser populations require more complex organization, more complex organization allows for ever-greater levels of food production—which in turn generates more population growth. Meanwhile, greater food surpluses allow for more specialization of non-producers and also provide the impetus for more expansion (as when farmers became soldiers in the off-season). This simple feedback loop forms the foundation of the development of human societies.

PART FOUR
AROUND THE WORLD
IN FIVE CHAPTERS

Now that we've heard Diamond's arguments about how and why the pace of history differed across the various continents, we visit each major continental group in turn and hear a complete history of each. In taking us on this journey, Diamond tests his theories and fills in any blanks he's left in his earlier discussions. The result is a comprehensive whirlwind tour of each of the world's main regions.

First, Diamond looks at the history of the peoples of Australia and New Guinea. As of 40,000 years ago, Australia and New Guinea were joined as a single land mass, populated throughout by peoples who were of Southeast Asian origin and had stone tools and primitive technologies. Australia and New Guinea became separated at the end of the Pleistocene Ice Ages (12,000–8,000 years ago) when melting ice caps washed over the land between them.

Over the thousands of years following, the societies of these two areas developed along very different paths: New Guineans adopted a number of technological advancements, while Australian peoples remained more primitive. As we might expect, the different environments they faced contributed to enormous differences in their societies. New Guinea, with its equatorial climate, heavy rainfall, and fertile volcanic soils, was able to support agriculture and higher population densities, at least in the higher elevations. Australia, in contrast, was—and is—among the hottest, driest, and least suitable agricultural climates in the world, able to support only nomadic, low-density populations.

Despite being first with stone tools, Australia and New Guinea never developed far beyond nomadic hunter-gathers—or, in the case of highland New Guinea, tribal farming societies. They simply lacked adequate resources to develop further. New Guinea had some crops suitable for agriculture, but they yielded little protein. Although pigs and chickens were introduced about 3,600 years ago, they were useless as beasts of burden, and were never numerous enough to provide large amounts of protein.

The hunter-gatherer lifestyle persisted for practical reasons. Even with denser populations than Australia, New Guinea never developed the densities required to evolve to higher levels of societal organization.

Australia's resources were even more limited. The soil was notably infertile and offered virtually no domesticable plants. No large mammals existed for domestication. Perhaps most important, the Australian continent was almost completely isolated from contact with other peoples, except for a few trading outposts on equally isolated islands in the Torres Strait (between Australia and New Guinea). Add to that the irregular cycles of unpredictable weather patterns characteristic of Australia, and it's no wonder that the continent remained a land of small bands of Aborigines with primitive levels of technology and farming.

The next stop on Diamond's world tour is China, one of the original sites where farming, domesticated animals, and written language first developed. When compared to the other areas where these developments began independently, China presents a key difference. Unlike these other areas, each of which is home to multiple peoples with different languages, China is far more homogeneous.

From very early on, China's history is one of unification. While other areas were still evolving into states, China was already coming together, as separate local cultures expanded, interacted, and coalesced. Eventually the "Chinese" displaced or conquered smaller groups within the region. Diamond relies heavily on linguistic evidence to show the ways in which smaller tribes were assimilated and lost their old languages.

This large, unified Chinese state, able to support large classes of workers, was the site of rapid technological advances. Major new inventions, from paper to gunpowder, from the wheelbarrow to the compass, originated in China. In short, the case of China provides an excellent example of the progression of human societies through population growth. As the various groups merged to form larger and larger states, the pace of bureaucracy and technological innovation increased until a single, homogenous empire emerged.

In Chapter 17, "Speedboat to Polynesia," Diamond returns us to the Pacific islands, where the accidents of environment are especially pronounced. During the course of human history on these islands, different ways of life evolved on different islands based solely on the resources available. Again, Diamond relies on complex linguistic theories to trace large-scale movements of people, mostly from mainland China to Indonesia, Java, and beyond—the so-called Austronesian expansion.

According to Diamond, the Austronesian expansion was "among the biggest population movements of the last 6,000 years," as significant as the movement of people from the Old World to the New. Compelling linguistic evidence tells the story of this expansion in vivid detail. Although the Austronesian expansion occurred centuries before the Eurasian conquering of the New World, the story is similar: groups of farmer-herders with food surpluses and political organization built boats to explore—and ultimately conquer—distant and not-so-distant islands.

The archaeological evidence suggests that the Austronesian expansion and the conquest of the New World were not only similar in nature but also in result. Natives of the conquered Pacific islands were killed, assimilated, or brutalized by imported infectious diseases. There was one notable exception, however. The advancing Austronesian invaders *didn't* succeed in taking over highland New Guinea, where the indigenous population remained in control. The difference was, of course, food production. At the time of the Austronesians' arrival, New Guinea already supported

"The different historical trajectories of Africa and Europe stem ultimately from differences in real estate."

dense populations of food producers who were able to integrate easily many of the new technologies the explorers brought (including domesticated pigs and chickens) without succumbing to their domination.

Diamond then returns us to the Americas with a comparison of the cultures of North and South America to those of their Eurasian conquerors. This overview of the major differences between the two continents as of 1492—and the ultimate causes behind them—stands as an excellent summary of all the major arguments in *Guns, Germs, and Steel*. Again, the ultimate differences stem from food production and animal domestication—two features of Eurasian society that were limited or nonexistent in the Americas. By now, Diamond's story is familiar and somewhat repetitive, but the scientific evidence behind it is still compelling.

The final stop on the world tour of human history is Africa, where humans have lived the longest and where the greatest human diversity can be found (Africa is home to five of the world's six major groups of humans).

In Africa, linguistic evidence is again critical to much of Diamond's argument, especially because many parts of Africa had no written language systems with which to record events. By combining linguistic evidence with the archaeological record, Diamond shows that the movement of peoples was directly related to food production. African peoples with food-producing capabilities engulfed and assimilated groups of hunter-gatherers in much the same way as on other continents. Africa's unique geography, bisected by the Sahara desert, has allowed small pockets of otherwise eradicated groups—Pygmies, for example—to remain.

As for the European conquest of sub-Saharan Africa, the collision of cultures played out in much the same way as it did in the European conquest of the Americas. Sub-Saharan Africa had few domesticable plants and no domesticable animals. Crops and technologies moved slowly, if at all, along the north-south axis of the continent. This geographic reality created a lag in the development of factors that might have led to guns, germs, and steel—providing Europe with an early advantage.

EPILOGUE
THE FUTURE OF HUMAN HISTORY AS A SCIENCE

A theory as enormous and all-encompassing as Diamond's is bound to leave a few loose ends. Diamond uses the Epilogue to tie these loose ends up and identify questions that can't be answered without further exploration. Among the issues that Diamond feels warrant more attention include deeper quantitative studies of plant and animal species and the factors that made them candidates for domestication, as well as examinations of powerful individuals and "cultural idiosyncrasies"—what he calls the "wild cards of history."

Perhaps more important, though, the Epilogue gives Diamond an opportunity to discuss the profound changes in methodology his work encourages. He argues that established scientific fields like paleontology and astronomy deal every day with the unknowns of history, and that his unique brand of historical study has much in common with these types of sciences. He maintains a fervent belief that a more collaborative, multi-disciplinary approach to all aspects of human history would make the larger patterns clearer and bring the rigors of science to bear on the "social sciences." This melding of science and history forms the heart of Diamond's mission the motivation behind the work we know as *Guns, Germs, and Steel*.

Too Good to Be True?

Diamond's book leaves us with one big question: has he hit the nail on the head or is his theory a massive oversimplification?

○ ○ ○

Diamond seems to use environment to explain everything. Don't religions, ideologies, and powerful individuals matter?

ALWAYS LOOK AT THE BIG PICTURE

Yes, great leaders and ideas have played critical roles in shaping human history—but their impact is greatest across smaller areas and shorter time frames. Diamond's subject is the entire globe across all of human history, a vast scope that minimizes the impact of any single person or group. While a powerful individual like Alexander the Great or Christopher Columbus may have influenced the course of Western history, their lives and accomplishments don't help us understand the *ultimate* causes that allowed people like them to exist in the first place. Diamond's focus on environments and ultimate causes always pushes back from the singular event to its preconditions, making individual people largely irrelevant to his study.

Diamond's concern is less with individuals or concepts than with the origins of the societies in which they arose. The question for him isn't how a prominent individual made a difference, but rather how the culture came to produce such an individual, what trends the individual represents, and what else happened around this individual. Diamond sums it up like this: "Perhaps Alexander the Great did nudge the course of western Eurasia's already literate, food-producing, iron-equipped states, but he had nothing to do with the fact that western Eurasia already supported literate, food-producing, iron-equipped states at a time when Australia still supported only non-literate hunter-gatherer tribes lacking metal tools."

Much of Diamond's work consciously (or unconsciously) deconstructs the myth of the Great Man. For example, in his discussion of Pizarro's capture of the Inca emperor Atahuallpa, Diamond points out that although Pizarro may have been a great leader, his victory was more a result of the smallpox germs that had already decimated much of the Inca empire than anything he did personally.

Inventors, too, in Diamond's view, are more the product of their environments than individual Great Men. Diamond's discussion of the processes of invention demonstrates that most inventions, rather than flashes of genius on the parts of individual people, have been improvements upon existing technologies. Although it's commonly accepted that James Watt invented the steam engine in 1769, in reality he modified a 1712 invention by Thomas Newcomen, which was itself an improvement on the 1698 work of Thomas Savery, and so on. Diamond rejects outright the idea that history would've been vastly different if a single inventor hadn't been born in a specific time and place. He argues that the pool of potential brilliant inventors is as vast as humanity—the factor that determines success isn't the individual but whether he can develop his talents. To do so, an inventor needs a sedentary, farm-based culture where people are able to develop non-portable possessions and classes of people are freed from food production to focus on other areas, such as new technologies. The fact that inventors don't arise among hunter-gatherers has more to do with their preoccupation with finding food than with any lack of intellectual potential.

Diamond doesn't pay much attention to the ways in which civilization gave rise to the big institutions that have come to exert a profound influence on society. He mentions religion only briefly, characterizing it as a byproduct of the development of ever larger and more centralized, bureaucratic states (kleptocracies, to use Diamond's word). According to Diamond, one way that kleptocrats were able to maintain authority and gather resources (think taxes) from people was by creating a religious ideology to support their demands.

A universally shared ideology binds members of the society together even when the group is too large to be bound by kinship. It gives leaders— often priests—justification to lead. It provides people with reasons to sacrifice themselves for others in wars of conquest (the Crusades, for example). Diamond's treatment of religion might seem far too simplistic for a human phenomenon that's driven so much cultural and political development in history. But when we push way, way back to ultimate causes, the specifics tend to fade into a larger question: under what *conditions* would these ideologies would be practical?

> Diamond doesn't totally reject the role of individuals in shaping history, but he refers to them as "history's wild cards."

Diamond doesn't totally reject the role of individuals and "cultural idiosyncrasies" in shaping history, but he refers to them as "history's wild cards"—mysteries that remain open after we account for environmental factors. In the time frame of millennia, these wild cards have little impact. But, as Diamond acknowledges, they're highly relevant for short term, localized histories. When we take the long view, individual efforts tend to blur into the larger trends, especially when the history in question is ancient. No matter how powerful an individual was in 1000 A.D., or how much territory he could control, he couldn't influence the whole world at once.

Modern history presents an entirely different challenge, however. In an era when events are broadcast all over the world as they occur, when an individual leader has the power to unleash mass destruction at the touch of a button, the question of the role of individuals is far more important. Diamond's rejection of individual agents of history works fine for an examination of the past 10,000 years—but it's problematic for the past hundred.

Why was the Fertile Crescent the origin of so many important developments in early history? Why was it Europe, instead, that ended up spreading its culture to the rest of the world?

LOCATION, LOCATION, LOCATION

Virtually every one of the advantages Diamond discusses in *Guns, Germs, and Steel* was present in the Fertile Crescent—the area of Southwest Asia that today includes Iraq, Iran, Syria, and Turkey—from the very beginning. The region had an extraordinary head start over much of the world. We can trace plant domestication back to 8500 B.C. and animal domestication to 8000 B.C., the earliest known dates for both phenomena.

Many of the first domesticated crops were native to the Fertile Crescent because of its climate. Most of the area lies in a Mediterranean climate zone marked by long, hot summers and mild, wet winters. Many useful plants in this zone are annuals, meaning their entire life cycle is just one year long. With only a year to live, annuals put most of their efforts into producing large seeds. These edible seeds are the "cereal crops" central to early farming and still dominant in the human diet—cereals are six of the twelve major world crops today. These large-seeded annuals are also so-called "selfers," meaning they self-pollinate instead of requiring another plant with which to reproduce. Selfers are far easier to domesticate because they generally make exact replicas of themselves. Because of this biological characteristic, farmers can predictably reproduce useful mutations in these crops.

These large-seeded, self-pollinating cereals grew wild in abundance and needed little modification to become crops, allowing an easy transition from hunter-gatherer to food-producing lifestyles in the Fertile Crescent. The transition was even easier because of the region's broad range of elevations, from the lowest point on earth (the Dead Sea) to a mountain tens of thousands of feet high. This variation meant that farmers could plant crops on hillsides and have them mature at different times, allowing for ongoing harvests over time rather than overwhelming single harvests that would require enormous resources.

The Fertile Crescent also happened to have several important mammals that were ideal for domestication. Southwest Asia is the first known site for domestication of the sheep and goat, and one of the first for the pig and cow. These are four of the so-called "major five" domesticated animals in the world (the horse being the fifth).

This combination of cereals with protein-rich animals created a nutritious diet for the Fertile Crescent's farmers and allowed for huge food surpluses. These conditions were ideal for the rise of dense, sedentary populations. As a result, people were free to specialize in non-farming jobs: inventors, scribes, soldiers, and managers of growing city-states. In short, the conditions in the Fertile Crescent provided the recipe for civilization as we've come to know it.

But although the Fertile Crescent began with a great head start and enjoyed the seat of world power for generations, it began to decline in importance as soon as its advantages spread to other regions. The most significant reason for this decline is ecological. As Diamond puts it, "Fertile Crescent and eastern Mediterranean societies had the misfortune to arise in an ecologically fragile environment. They committed ecological suicide by destroying their own resource base." The climate, so ideal for growing annual cereal crops, yielded too little rainfall to allow vegetation to regrow fast enough, especially in areas where farmers had let their animals overgraze. Forests that had been cleared for agriculture never grew back. Without the cover of trees and grass, erosion became a major problem. Extensive irrigation caused salt to accumulate. These problems persisted so long that today the area formerly known as the Fertile Crescent is largely unfarmable. Years of overuse have transformed the entire region into desert and eroded landscapes. Without oil as an economic base, many of the countries in the region would face serious poverty and hunger.

Europe acquired virtually all of its agricultural materials and techniques from the Fertile Crescent. In fact, none of the major domesticated plants or animals in Europe were domesticated locally. After adopting the Fertile Crescent's advantages—its crops, technologies, and domesticated animals—Europe was able to quickly make the most of them. Because of its hardier climate and more generous rainfall, Europe was (and still is) able to sustain intensive farming and herding without significant erosion or regrowth problems.

So even with a late start, Europe's environment was better able to support agriculture—but that's not the only reason it pulled ahead of the Fertile Crescent and eventually launched the ships that brought guns, germs, and steel to the rest of the world. Europe's fractured, competitive states made use of their resources by encouraging experimentation and risk-taking. With a strong merchant class and capitalist economy, Europe sent explorers as much to find fortune as to satisfy curiosity. Patent laws encouraged and protected inventors and explorers, embracing their discoveries with a culture of inquiry. And regardless of local authority, individual governments were limited in the power they could wield over a geographically and linguistically divided continent. In short, Europe was a culture intent on discovery. It has a long history of borrowing the best advantages from the sites of their origin—like agriculture from the Fertile Crescent—and improving upon them.

In his Epilogue, Diamond acknowledges the need to apply his interdisciplinary methods to shorter time frames and smaller regions. He cites Europe's eclipsing of the Fertile Crescent as one such case study that needs further examination. Given that many of his best explanations for Europe's rise are cultural or political causes and not necessarily ultimate causes—the "reasons behind the reasons"—this extra research would be interesting and valuable.

○ ○ ○

Why is Diamond so interested in the idea of east-west axes and north-south axes? Why is east-west an advantage and north-south a disadvantage? Is it really that important?

CHANGES IN LATITUDES, CHANGES IN ATTITUDES

As Diamond shows us, big human innovations like farming, the domestication of animals, and the development of writing systems happened independently in only a few places. These technologies only showed up in other regions when those regions came into contact with peoples who already had the technologies. Proximity and access to the areas where technologies first arose was critical because it determined how soon a region could adopt or modify a tool or technique. In short, ease of travel and contact between cultures was an enormous contributing factor in the development of guns, germs, and steel. Ultimately, geography was a major deciding factor in this diffusion of technologies.

When we look at a map of the world, we're immediately struck by the differences in orientation of the different continents. The large landmass of Eurasia is largely east-west, with few natural barriers across its long axis. But Africa and the Americas are oriented north-south. As a result, Diamond points out, much of Eurasia lies along the same latitudes and enjoys a similar climate: "Portugal, northern Iran, and Japan, all located at about the same latitude but lying successively 4,000 miles east or west of each other, are more similar to each other in climate than each is to a location lying even a mere 1,000 miles due south." This band of similar climates stretches more than 8,000 miles from Ireland to Japan, creating the longest land distance on Earth.

In contrast, the width of the Americas varies from 3,000 miles at the widest point to just 40 miles in Panama. The climates of the different latitudes of the north-south oriented Americas vary greatly, from the arctic plains of Canada to the tropics of Brazil and everything in between. These different regions, though all within the Americas, are suited to completely different crop cycles.

Crops can only spread across areas that share similar climates, where day lengths, soil conditions, seasons, and average temperatures are all similar. Crops that require certain conditions to grow could be planted in new areas along the same latitude and probably thrive right away.

In this way, the Fertile Crescent's "founder package" of crops easily made its way across the east-west axis of Eurasia. Crops that originated elsewhere along the axis spread back to the center as well. By 2,000 years ago, the Roman Empire was feeding itself on a variety of foods brought from all over Eurasia. Domesticated animals also were able to spread easily along the east-west axis for the same reasons. Animals and the foods they ate thrived in specific climates and not in others. Tools and technologies spread along the same east-west route, for they were often related to the food packages being adopted. Carts and plows might accompany cattle, for example.

The north-south axis of the Americas, on the other hand, presented a large handicap. We see a good example in the fate of a specific animal—the llama. Llamas were domesticated in the Andes by 3000 B.C. At roughly the same time, the wheel was in wide use to the north, in Central America. Even though the Andes and Central America are only 1,200 miles apart, an area of hot, steamy rainforest—where llamas can't thrive—separates them. Indeed, even 5,000 years later, llamas still weren't hitched up to wheels.

Other geographic features handicapped the Americas as well, so that even the widest areas of shared latitude had significant barriers. The southeast and southwest regions of the United States are at the same latitude, and crops from one region could easily have grown in the other. But diffusion was slow because so much of the area between them—Texas and the southern Plains—was too dry for agriculture. And the Rocky Mountains in North America and Andes in South America proved formidable boundaries that isolated groups from each other for thousands of years.

Eurasia, in contrast, has virtually no barriers along most of its east-west axis. Crops, domesticated animals, and technologies such as written language and iron tools spread easily from one end of the land mass to another. Along the way, they were adopted by native populations or, in many cases, introduced by conquering groups. In fact, this diffusion occurred so quickly that scientists studying the spread of farming through Europe around 5400 B.C. discovered agricultural sites all the way from Poland to Holland that were nearly contemporaneous. In marked contrast, Mexican corn, squash, and beans took thousands of years to reach the southwest United States, just 700 miles away.

Why are domesticated animals such an advantage? With so many large mammals in the wild, why have only a few species ever been domesticated?

PLOWS, PROTEIN, AND PATHOGENS

Domesticated animals offered a huge advantage for societies that had them, enabling a given society to develop many of the most important factors for the rise of advanced civilizations. Large animals that served as beasts of burden greatly increased farming productivity. By harnessing animals to plows, farmers could cultivate far more land than they could with hand tools. They could work heavier soils that required deeper digging. Animal manure also fertilized the soil and provided fuel. Animals used for food yielded high-quality protein as well as regular supplies of milk, wool, and eggs. In short, domesticated animals meant more food and material surpluses—which in turn could support higher population densities and free more people from food production, enabling them to become inventors, scribes, and soldiers.

Horses, originally domesticated in western Asia, represented a particularly big advantage. Horses provided mobility, speed, and a tremendous edge in battle. When people with horses fought people without them—as in Pizarro's massacre of the Incas—the result was nearly always a lopsided victory for the horsemen. Riders could attack by surprise and escape quickly. The terror that horses inspired in people who had never seen them before often provided an advantage as well.

But perhaps domesticated animals' biggest contributions to human history were the epidemic diseases that evolved from germs present in the animals. Immunity to these diseases was the biggest advantage herders had over hunter-gatherers. Living in dense population centers and in close proximity to animals and their germs, herders evolved immunity to epidemic diseases of animal origin. Hunter-gathers, on the other hand, lacked these immunities and died in droves after exposure, virtually guaranteeing the successful expansion of farmers and their culture.

Knowing the clear advantages of domesticating animals, ancient peoples domesticated every possible candidate animal. But the number of species that were suitable was only a tiny fraction of the overall pool of large mammals. In fact, only fourteen of the world's 148 potentially suitable big mammals (those larger than 100 pounds) were ever successfully domesticated. These included the "major five" that became widespread—cows, sheep, goats, pigs, and horses—and the "minor nine" that remained useful only in limited areas—reindeer, donkeys, Arabian camels, Bactrian camels, yaks, llamas, Bali cattle, water buffalo, and guar. All but the llama were native to some part of Eurasia, providing one of the biggest advantages for history's luckiest location.

In 10,000 years of human history, no new domesticated large mammals have been introduced.

Why weren't other animals candidates? Did people just need time to figure out how to domesticate them? In 10,000 years of human history, no new domesticated large mammals have been introduced. Humans have been able to harness and train additional species, such as African and Asian elephants—but these are captured and tamed, not bred in captivity. Modern zoos are technically able to "domesticate" many species, but they haven't created any economically viable species for herding.

So few species have been domesticated because animals must meet several very specific criteria to be suitable candidates. Failure to meet a single requirement disqualifies an animal completely. First, the animal must eat a diet that humans can provide. This eliminates carnivores, for the effort to raise or hunt meat to feed a meat-eater would be more than the potential benefit the animal could provide. Similarly, animals that need specific, difficult-to-grow plants for their diet are poor candidates. Providing special types of eucalyptus trees to feed koala bears would diminish their usefulness as domesticated animals.

Animals also must be willing and able to breed in captivity if they're to be domesticated. Their courtship rituals can't be too elaborate or demand too much space. For instance, this requirement eliminated the cheetah, which wasn't successfully bred in captivity until 1960, despite thousands of years of effort. In order to mate, cheetah males need to chase females for several days over long distances. And once bred, animals need to reach maturity quickly to justify the effort and food put into raising them. Gorillas, which take about twelve years to reach maturity, are a poor choice.

An animal's disposition is an important factor too. Animals that bite, spit, or kick are unsuitable, as are truly violent ones, like grizzly bears, African buffaloes, and hippos, which kill more people every year than lions. Other animals that are too nasty and unpredictable to domesticate include zebras, as well as six of the eight species of wild horses. A tendency to panic when closed in is another disqualifier—one that eliminates most species of deer, along with gazelles, which bash themselves to death against fences when penned in.

Finally, animals have to live under social structures that make it possible for humans to domesticate them. They need to live in large groups or herds year round. Some animals, such as the antelope, live mostly in herds but become fiercely territorial during their breeding season. Not surprisingly, we can't domesticate them. Herds also need to be tolerant of other herds within their territories in order to behave in captivity. Farmers must be able to pen two herds together. And herds need to have a well-maintained hierarchy of dominance that humans can take over. The shepherd who leads a herd is actually taking the role of the dominant alpha sheep—this is what enables one individual to drive a whole herd.

Only a very few animal species meet all these criteria at once, so only a very few were successfully domesticated—mostly in Eurasia. Africa, Australia, and North America had no suitable candidates at all. The readiness to adopt domesticated animals when they were introduced (as the North American Indians adopted horses) suggests that the people on these three continents understood the value of domesticating animals and would surely have done it themselves if they could.

Why were Eurasian germs so much of a threat to people in the Americas? Why wasn't there a threat to Eurasians from germs native to America?

BLAME OUR FOUR-LEGGED FRIENDS

When Eurasians came to the Americas, the result was devastating for the natives, who died in huge numbers from lethal germs that the invaders unwittingly brought with them. In some areas, native populations diminished by as much as 95 percent. The simple reason for this is that Eurasians had lived with domesticated animals for tens of thousands of years while the Native Americans had not. Living in proximity to animals gave Eurasians immunity to diseases of animal origin. This would prove to be their biggest advantage.

We can trace nearly every major crowd-borne epidemic disease in human history to domesticated herd animals. Influenza originated with pigs, measles and tuberculosis with cattle, and so on. What began as animal illnesses evolved over time to also attack nearby humans, eventually resulting in uniquely human epidemic diseases.

Diseases evolve from animals to humans through a four-stage process. In the first stage, there are diseases humans occasionally pick up through direct contact with animals, either domestic or in the wild. These are still strictly animal diseases. Their transfer to humans is rare, and they can't be transmitted from human to human. In the second stage, an animal disease evolves to attack humans and cause epidemics in which it spreads from human to human. But at this stage, the epidemic dies out after affecting everyone in an area and never returns. There are many of these mysterious epidemics throughout history, with names like the "English sweating sickness" that affected Europe at the turn of the sixteenth century. The third stage involves former animal diseases that have moved to humans and are still evolving. AIDS, which evolved from a disease in African monkeys, is a prime example. Though AIDS was discovered in humans only as recently as 1959, it's already evolved into a global epidemic. The fourth and final stage in disease evolution is the established major epidemics—cholera, smallpox, measles, and so on—that have predictable patterns and now affect only humans.

In crowd epidemics, such as those Europe experienced in the Middle Ages, disease spread rapidly and infected virtually everyone in a densely populated area. Then, when the disease had no one left to infect, it died out—at least until it was reintroduced to attack children born since the last epidemic. The people who survived these epidemics were those with the most resistant genes. As the only ones left, they passed their resistant genes on to new generations, increasing the chances for the group's overall resistance. These evolutionary adaptations allowed European explorers to breathe deadly germs in the faces of New World natives while they themselves were unaffected.

Epidemic diseases require two conditions to take hold. First, they occur in dense populations, where people live in close proximity and microbes can easily spread. Second, because they originate with animal hosts, they can only develop in places where people live among animals. Although primitive societies in the Americas were often densely populated, there were no domesticated animals. As a result, no animal diseases and human immunities could evolve. With none of the immunity that comes with proximity to animals, the New World natives were doomed.

"Far more Native Americans died in bed from Eurasian germs than on the battlefield from European guns and swords."

The devastation imported germs brought to the Americas was staggering. In the hundred years following its introduction in Mexico, smallpox reduced the native Mexican population from 20 million to just 1.6 million. Germs that Spanish explorers brought to the American coast made their way inland, wiping out densely populated areas along the Mississippi River before the explorers themselves ever arrived. When Hernando de Soto arrived to explore the Mississippi delta, he found abandoned towns all along the river where every single person had died.

We might wonder why the densely populated empires of the Americas didn't develop any of their own epidemic germs. Some scholars believe that syphilis may have originated in the Americas. If true, it would be the only native American disease. Nonetheless, the question remains as to where these germs would've come from. Without domesticated animals to provide microbes, there was simply no source for the germs. Also, the dense population centers of the Americas developed later than those in Eurasia. And these American population centers remained fairly isolated from one another, with limited contact and trade that would have furthered the rapid spread of any diseases—a sharp contrast with the teeming trade routes of Eurasia, where germs were traded along with crops, technologies, and animals.

Although Eurasians faced no germs in the Americas, diseases like malaria and yellow fever stopped them when they attempted to colonize tropical areas of Africa, New Guinea, India, and Southeast Asia. In all of these areas, local populations enjoyed similar immunities. These pockets of tropical climate were the only areas that could avoid domination by invading Eurasians, at least initially.

○ ○ ○

Why did China become politically unified while Europe remained a collection of competing states? What consequences did this difference have for human history?

THE TORTOISE AND THE HARE

This key difference between China and Europe stemmed from differences in the timing of major cultural developments and differences in the geographical features of the two regions. China had a long head start on much of Europe in food production and the social and technological changes food production brought. Also, the geography of mainland China offers few barriers to the spread of crops and innovations. Europe, in contrast, wasn't among the first sites for food production—it received crop packages later from the Fertile Crescent. And Europe's geography is fragmented, with mountains and ragged coastlines creating pockets of different ethnicities and cultures.

China began the cycles of cultural development early. It moved quickly from food production and animal domestication to dense population centers and empire building. The physical environment in China provided ideal conditions for rapid growth. Ecological diversity and suitable climate conditions allowed for the domestication of a variety of crops and animals. Two major rivers—the Yellow and the Yangtze—connect the broad expanse of China's heartland east-west. These rivers carried new foods and innovations quickly and developed into two large core areas of high productivity. Then, canals joined the two rivers and created a unified central area.

> While disunity may have caused Europe to lag behind China initially, it eventually gave Europe a lasting advantage.

Eventually, most of the Chinese mainland was united in common language and political organization. This structured, organized society allowed China to take the lead in technology, inventing a staggering number of major technologies—cast iron, gunpowder, paper, printing, and notably, seagoing ships. Fleets of hundreds of Chinese sailing ships traveled across the Indian Ocean to Africa decades before Europeans left for the New World.

But the political unity of China was also its undoing, for it caused China to lose many of its head-start advantages. For example, the fleets of Chinese ships that voyaged in the early fifteenth century had sailed under the banner of a political faction that later lost power. The new leaders that stepped in wanted nothing to do with the old leaders' projects, so they forbade shipping and shipbuilding. Because the entire Chinese region was politically unified, this one decision became complete and permanent. In short, one voice could speak for all of China, for better or worse. When the new edict was passed, no shipyards remained to take up building again at a later time. Individuals who wanted to explore the seas had nowhere to turn for support.

Europe never became unified like China. While this disunity may have caused Europe to lag behind China initially, it eventually gave Europe a lasting advantage. Europe's geography makes a Chinese-style unification impossible. Europe is split into five large peninsulas and two large islands, all sufficiently isolated to make dominance of one over the others impossible. Mountain ranges bisect the interior of the continent, and the main river systems (the Rhine and Danube) are smaller and cover less of the total land mass than China's main rivers. These environmental conditions caused Europe to develop multiple, independent centers of population and political organization that existed alongside one another in constant competition.

These adjacent, competing societies in Europe created ideal conditions for technological innovation. Even when a given area rejected an invention or idea, that invention could easily make its way to another state that might be more receptive to it. No one voice could speak for all of Europe, so no developments could ever be put down completely. When explorers wanted to set out in ships from Europe, they had many leaders to appeal to for support. Columbus, for instance, met with rejection when he appealed for backing to the leaders of France and Portugal—but then found support in Spain. Had he been in China, there would've been one government, and only one, to ask.

The path of history would've been radically different if China hadn't been unified or if Europe had been. We could even argue that if environmental conditions were reversed, it might've been fragmented Chinese states that conquered the New World rather than European ones. Diamond gives us a compelling geographical explanation, but we might also argue that geographical conditions alone didn't guarantee that China would follow exactly the path it took.

Unlike many of the other areas of the world Diamond studies, China seems to offer the possibility that individuals and their actions can have a great impact, even in the long term. Certainly China's environment made unification possible, just as Europe's made it impossible. But what if the new leadership that took power in fifteenth-century China had decided to step up the pace of shipbuilding and exploration rather than shut it down? Would the New World be speaking Chinese rather than English, Spanish, French, and Portuguese? We'll never know for sure.

Why does Diamond say that human races are equal in intelligence but also that New Guineans might be genetically more intelligent? Isn't this a contradiction?

IT'S ENVIRONMENT, NOT RACE

Diamond generally rejects the idea of a genetic basis for intelligence, but he does allow that environmental conditions can influence human evolution over time, creating different tendencies and capabilities among peoples in different environments. So in effect, he *does* accept the idea of a genetic influence on intelligence—he just denies any specifically racial component. Following this logic, any human in a similar environment would evolve the same intellectual traits over time. The key factor here isn't inherent racial makeup but the theory of natural selection, under which certain genetic traits are favored for survival in certain environments. Just as an ability to withstand a very hot climate would be a naturally selected trait near the equator, so the ability to think in certain ways would be an evolutionarily useful trait in certain places.

The most notable example is Diamond's argument that the natives of New Guinea, far from being ignorant savages, are in fact highly intelligent—perhaps even smarter than the average Westerner. His reasoning goes like this: Westerners live in dense population centers where the most likely cause of death has typically been from infectious epidemic diseases. Therefore, survival for Westerners has depended mostly on resistance to these diseases. So Europeans who survived epidemics passed on their genes to future generations regardless of their relative intelligence. Natural selection for survival in Europe favored particular types of body chemistry, not intelligence.

Meanwhile, primitive hunter-gatherer societies have no such epidemic diseases. Survival depends on finding adequate food and avoiding murder, tribal warfare, and accidents. Natural selection has therefore favored individuals with intelligence and cunning. These survivors pass on their genetic material. In primitive societies, argues Diamond, intelligence is the most important trait for survival. These are the genes most likely to be passed on, making the average primitive more likely to be highly intelligent.

He furthers his argument by pointing out that modern-day New Guineans also avoid the "developmental disadvantages" that have stemmed from Westerners' use of passive forms of entertainment. In contrast to Western children who watch multiple hours of television each day, children in New Guinea spend most of their time in active play, which helps them develop intelligence and social skills.

Diamond goes to great lengths to show that the differences between modern industrialized societies and those that remain behind are in no way due to lower intelligence among primitives. This point is critical to his overall argument and to a larger desire for understanding and an end to racism. But to suggest that there's an intellectual inequality that favors the primitives is perhaps too much. By opening the door to allow for the idea that intelligence can be a genetic trait, Diamond weakens the rest of his argument—especially since he doesn't seem to hold the door open long enough to allow everyone to walk through it. He's more effective when he sticks to an environmental focus, analyzing the suitability of intellectual traits to a particular environment and avoiding declarations of inherent "absolute" states of intelligence.

Diamond detracts from his argument by not extending it to everyone. For example, if wild, natural environments created an evolutionary tendency toward specific intelligences among "primitives" in Australia and New Guinea, shouldn't it stand to reason that urban, industrial environments have also created tendencies toward other types of intelligence? Without judging which types of intelligence are "better," it seems there should be room to at least acknowledge them. But Diamond doesn't. In the end, it seems unbalanced to acknowledge the effects of some environments but not others.

Clearly, Diamond makes this argument to provoke Westerners into thinking differently about so-called "primitive" people. His goal is admirable, but in arguing that natural selection has created a higher level of intelligence in a group of people, he seems to do exactly what he claims to oppose—namely, to assess intelligence based on race and genetics.

Many people assume that Aboriginal Australians must be truly "primitive" because white settlers were able to "tame" the continent in only a few generations, while Aborigines still had only Stone Age technologies. How is this thinking flawed?

THE EUROPEANS DIDN'T EXACTLY PACK LIGHT

Although racist explanations for the differences among cultures began to fall out of favor long before *Guns, Germs, and Steel,* it seems Aboriginal Australians have continued to be an exception. In Diamond's view, people who wouldn't dare generalize about the intelligence of other groups have had difficulty resisting racial generalizations about Aborigines. Diamond conjectures that perhaps it's a matter of appearance: Aborigines tend to have markedly different facial structures from other ethnic groups, and for many years were considered a possible "missing link" between humans and apes. Or perhaps it's the Aborigines' extreme isolation and small numbers. They live in remote areas within a larger remote area, and few white Australians have any regular contact with them.

Diamond believes that this lack of meaningful interaction makes it easier to mythologize about Aboriginal culture, to guess at what they think and do. In addition, their lifestyle remains impossible for most "advanced" cultures to understand. They rely on ancient tools and rituals, despite the availability of modern technologies to them today. This mode of living is baffling to many modern Australians, some of whom conclude that Aborigines must simply be inferior.

It's important to remember too that the inferiority of another race has long been offered as a rationalization for enslavement and genocide. White settlers in Australia, as in North America, found it much easier to rationalize the removal of native populations that they could consider "savages." White Australia has only recently begun to reexamine its history with regard to the Aborigines and to acknowledge the wrongs that were committed. It's this process that ultimately allows for the reconsidering of racist explanations.

One argument often used to justify this racist attitude toward Aborigines is that white settlers in Australia established a flourishing modern civilization—agriculture, cities, and technologies—in only a few generations, while the native population made virtually no progress in these areas in 40,000 years. The explanation that the white settlers were superior is inevitable, especially when also politically convenient.

But this idea is simply untrue. Yes, white settlers were able to establish European-style culture in a short time, but they didn't invent or domesticate anything within Australia. Virtually every single advantage they enjoyed was imported from Europe. They didn't arrive in a virgin land and "tame" it—they brought with them the fruits of 10,000 years of culture and technology: plants and seeds, domesticated animals, written language, political organization, weapons, tools, and so on. There were still no native Australian plants suitable for domestication, and the Europeans didn't discover any new ones there. Instead, they brought their own. Certainly they faced a great deal of hardship in the new land, but they did so armed with the full complement of guns, germs, and steel that would allow them to dominate Australia and its natives.

The **clash** between **Aboriginal** Australians and **the** white settlers who replaced them is **typical** of history's clashes between haves and have-nots.

The clash between Aboriginal Australians and the white settlers who replaced them is typical of history's clashes between haves and have-nots. Aboriginal hunter-gatherers occupied the most fertile and productive lands. Because these lands were best suited to agriculture, white settlers sought to remove the natives through any means necessary. As in other regions of the world, it was Eurasian germs that did most of the removal work, with Aborigines in droves dying of diseases like smallpox, influenza, and tuberculosis.

Diamond goes to great lengths to point out that Aborigines, far from being less intelligent than whites, in fact possess a very different type of intelligence—one that's adapted to their environment. He argues quite effectively that if white settlers were in fact so superior, we would've seen them flourish in the Australian wild as well. But without their imported cargo to sustain them, white settlers were nearly universally doomed in the bush.

Australian history is filled with these stories. The desert town of Menindee is famous as the base camp from which Robert Burke and William Wills set out to explore Australia from north to south. Despite having six camels and food for three months, they ran out of provisions just north of Menindee and only survived when a group of well-fed, thriving Aborigines, able to find all the food and water they needed in the desert, rescued them. After Burke shot his pistol and scared the Aborigines into fleeing, it was only a month until Burke and Wills died of starvation, unable to survive on their own. A few days in the heat and dust of the outback has killed many a hardy explorer, yet Aborigines have survived in the outback for tens of thousands of years. Clearly they possess a unique set of skills that allow them to survive the seemingly unsurvivable.

Yet while we can appreciate the Aborigines' unique intelligence and adaptation, the question still lingers: why didn't they move beyond the Stone Age? The answer, by now familiar, is simple: environment, environment, environment. We must recall the cycle of ultimate causes that lead to guns, germs, and steel. The onset of farming and domesticated animals creates sedentary lifestyles, population densities, specialized groups within society, language, politics, technology, and so on. Simply put, Australia just couldn't get started. It couldn't support the cycle because the environment offered no native domesticable plants and animals. The harsh and unpredictable climate yielded just enough sustenance to support small bands of hunter-gatherers. And Australia's isolation prevented the adoption of crops and technologies seen all over Eurasia. The Aborigines' contact with the outside world was limited to trade with villagers in islands of the Torres Strait. While these islanders were somewhat more advanced than Aborigines, and did introduce some innovations, Aborigines didn't encounter modern tools and methods until the British arrived in 1788. And by then, it would be too late to adopt or assimilate.

Diamond claims that technologies build upon one another to reinforce the conditions for each new development—a process he calls "autocatalytic." How does this process take place? How does it create even greater advantages for those with a head start?

BABY STEPS LEAD TO GIANT STEPS

In an autocatalytic system, the output of one process becomes the input for another. One finished product becomes the raw material for the next. Because development is exponential, the process speeds up over time, so that an early start yields much faster growth.

The development of iron-ore metallurgy provides a clear example of how this process works over time. Each advance on the path to extracting and working iron depended on the mastery of a previous process. The first ironworkers based their efforts on thousands of years of experience working with softer metals that required less heat to melt, as well as thousands of years experimenting with furnaces—first for pottery and later for working bronze.

When the fruits of these earlier developments came together, the Iron Age began in Eurasia. But Stone Age hunter-gatherers in Australia had no exposure to the technology or similar early steps. They couldn't begin to make iron tools simply because they were now being made in other parts of the world. Eurasia's head start thus became even greater, as iron smelting paved the way for still other major technologies, like guns, steam engines, automobiles, and so on.

Because technology develops cumulatively, having a head start—not just in a specific technology but in the overall movement from hunter-gatherer to farming lifestyles—was a critical factor in the pace of technological developments. The earlier a group established a sedentary agricultural lifestyle, the earlier it diversified social functions to create a class of people who were freed from food production and could focus on technologies. The development of complex technologies is also much easier for people who can remain in one place while working on an invention and don't need to carry the project with them as they travel in search of food. The earlier these conditions were present, the sooner societies could reach milestones like written language, metallurgy, and so on. It's therefore not surprising to find that most new, radical technologies arose in regions where food production began the earliest—namely, China and the Fertile Crescent.

Inventions didn't have to happen locally, though. Regions that were adjacent to places where technologies began could benefit from discoveries and inventions by simply adopting them. This was the case with the diffusion of early farming technologies from the Fertile Crescent to Europe. The entire package of crops spread to Europe, along with the tools and wheeled transport that made them practical. This diffusion came easiest along well-traveled routes, especially the major rivers of China and the east-west axis of Eurasia. Once again, location was critical to getting new technologies into the hands of inventors who could build upon them.

The rise and spread of technologies also depended on the conditions of the societies in which they developed. A new invention that took advantage of other inventions that enhanced its performance could be explosive for a society's rate of change. But a similar invention in a society lacking the other necessary factors would often languish.

A fascinating example of this phenomenon is the contrast between the Phaistos disc and Gutenberg's printing press. The Phaistos disc was a small clay disc discovered in 1908 at the excavation of a palace at Phaistos on the island of Crete. The disc is covered with an as-yet-undeciphered set of symbols, each one painstakingly pressed into the clay with a specially formed stamp. Dating from 1700 B.C., it's the earliest printed document in the world and remains the biggest mystery in the history of technology.

Although the Phaistos disc represents a huge leap of sophistication in the development of printing, no other examples of the technology have ever appeared anywhere else—indicating that it never became widespread. This makes sense when we consider the society and era it came from. In ancient Crete, only a few scribes would have had any use for the disc, which would've been labor intensive to create and offered little advantage over writing by hand. Other technologies of the era were limited, so the creator of the disc wasn't able to simplify or enhance his invention with other breakthroughs. As a result, it was never adopted.

Gutenberg's invention of the printing press in 1455 A.D. had a vastly different effect. Gutenberg's press took advantage of many other technologies that, when recombined, created an explosive new tool in a society that was ripe for it. Gutenberg used six major existing technologies to create his own: paper, the concept of moveable type (from China), presses originally developed for making wine and oil, metallurgic developments in working with steel and lead, an alphabet developed over millennia that required only a few different symbols to be cast, and a long history of trial and error in creating inks.

This prior diffusion of technologies created an environment where Gutenberg's was welcome. His achievement was to use each of these technologies in a new way. The creator of the Phaistos disc, on the other hand, had no such body of inventions to draw upon. Plus, a large population of literate Europeans welcomed Gutenberg's printed materials—an impetus for development that ancient Crete lacked.

○　○　○

In the end, when we look at winners and losers—at which cultures thrived and which were annihilated—was the determining factor just plain old luck?

A GAME OF CHANCE

In short, Diamond's conclusion is that where people were and where they could migrate to determined their fates more than anything else. We can sum up the course of history for different societies with the classic real estate phrase, "Location, location, location." Geographic location determined virtually everything for human groups, beginning with what plants and animals were available for domestication (if any) and the resulting possibility for evolving dense, specialized agricultural societies. Location also governed proximity to other cultures, which could bring these advantages to areas that lacked them, as well as the vulnerability of some regions to the conquering advances of others.

To have ready, local access to domesticable plants was the single most important advantage in Diamond's analysis—and in this sense, the luck of location was everything. Only a few locations, most notably the Fertile Crescent and China, happened to have indigenous plants that were suitable for domestication. The transition from a hunter-gatherer to a sedentary farming lifestyle—the first step down the path to civilization's advantages—occurred first in these fortunate places.

A people lucky enough to develop agriculture could then increase in numbers, with food surpluses to support different social groups. Freed from the need to find their own food, classes of merchants, inventors, soldiers, and bureaucrats emerged and furthered the development of sophisticated technology and political organization. This self-perpetuating cycle encouraged further growth of technology.

But while relatively dense and stratified societies developed everywhere that agriculture did, domesticable animals were the factor that allowed a society to get to the next level of development. With animals, a culture was able to grow even faster, benefiting from animal protein, wool and skins, milk, and animal labor. But most important, keepers of animals developed immunity to diseases. When technologically advanced peoples then set out to explore and conquer other areas, it was disease that ultimately allowed them to take over. Even fortunate, sophisticated empires in the Americas, who lacked only domesticated animals, saw their luck run out when faced with imported germs.

A region that lacked domesticable plants and animals could still develop the factors for success—if they were lucky enough to be located near the places where these factors evolved, and if they could adopt them quickly. Lucky meant being on the same landmass at a similar latitude, with no significant geographical barriers. Unlucky meant being on an island far from any other cultures or on the far side of a mountain range. Many areas of Europe that lacked native plants and animals were fortunate enough to adopt them quickly as they spread from the Fertile Crescent. In contrast, peoples like the Aboriginal Australians had no contact with any culture that might introduce them.

Although Diamond looks at the biggest picture in determining which areas had the biggest advantages, luck was a factor on a smaller scale as well. Individual encounters and decisions often had lucky or unlucky consequences. For example, it was ultimately unlucky for China that it ceased all shipbuilding and sea exploration in the fifteenth century. This decision was lucky for Europe, however, for it then took the world lead in exploration, collecting colonies and resources as a result.

Certainly effort and hard work had a place in securing success for individual groups. But looking at the broadest trends, the random distribution of advantages is still critical. No matter how great the conquerors of the New World were at fighting, their victories were mostly the result of luck. Their luck likely would've been much different if their adversaries weren't already dying of disease.

The Professor of Everything

If anyone's qualified to take a stab at an all-encompassing theory of history, the well-traveled, well-studied Diamond is it.

○   ○   ○

JARED DIAMOND IS FIRST AND FOREMOST an educator. A professor of physiology at the UCLA School of Medicine, he has taught there since 1966. Diamond provides us with a unique brand of scholarship: while much of his study is extremely specific (the evolution of individual bird species in New Guinea, for example), his overall knowledge is both broad and deep. His approach to the great questions of science and history is practical and interdisciplinary, drawing on both his own and other scholars' work in a variety of subject areas. He is in many ways a true Renaissance man, using knowledge gained in one area to enhance our understanding in another. Diamond doesn't believe in the artificial boundaries between the sciences and the humanities. He sees no reason why we shouldn't bring scientific methods to bear on questions of history and culture. This clever synthesis of seemingly unrelated disciplines is the foundation for the success of the arguments he makes in *Guns, Germs, and Steel*.

Born in 1937 in Boston and raised amid a family of scholars, Diamond was drawn early to the joys of learning and studying. His mother was a teacher and linguist, while his father was a professor of pediatrics at Harvard who specialized in the genetics of childhood illnesses. Diamond's early education at Roxbury Latin School focused on history, writing, and languages—subjects that he continued to study, in addition to sciences, as an undergraduate at Harvard University. He earned a bachelor's degree in biochemical sciences from Harvard in 1958.

Diamond initially meant to go on to practice medicine but decided instead to specialize in biological research, earning a Ph.D. in physiology from Cambridge University in 1961. After post-doctoral work in Europe, Diamond returned to Harvard in 1962 for research, becoming an associate in biophysics in 1965. He joined UCLA Medical School in 1966 as an associate professor of Physiology, and became a full professor in 1968.

Not surprisingly, Diamond's passions have influenced his work as much as his formal training. A self-described "fanatical" bird-watcher since the age of seven, he spends about a third of his time studying birds. His love of bird-watching led him to a parallel career in ornithology and environmental conservation, which has brought him repeatedly to the islands of New Guinea. Over the past four decades years, he has organized no fewer than seventeen expeditions to New Guinea to conduct fieldwork. One of the most notable discoveries of his birding career was the rediscovery of the golden-fronted bowerbird, which he encountered in a remote mountain range. Previously, the bird had only been seen in specimens found in a feather shop in nineteenth-century Paris.

Diamond's time in his "beloved New Guinea" also led him to develop a great love for the people of the island, which is evident in his interest in anthropology and his calling to write *Guns, Germs, and Steel* (to answer "Yali's Question"). This affinity is evident also in his treatment of the place these so-called New Guinean "primitives" have in human history. His connection to New Guinea, where so much of the diversity of the natural world can be found, has also led him to head up numerous committees to help design and implement a nature reserve system and various conservation policies for the island nation.

Much of Diamond's scientific research has focused on the fields of evolutionary biology and biogeography. He has extensively studied the

Seeing green

A committed conservationist, Diamond developed a national parks plan for New Guinea, which the New Guinean government adopted almost in its entirety. More generally, Diamond's groundbreaking work in relating the extinction rates of species to the size of their habitats has made a significant impact on the field of conservation biology and the creation of large nature reserves around the world.

ways in which human physiology, through natural selection, has developed to meet the demands the environment has placed on humans. One of Diamond's many important contributions to evolutionary science is a series of papers he has produced on the evolution of human genetic diseases, such as Tay-Sachs and diabetes. His interest in evolutionary biology has also contributed enormously to the development of interdisciplinary methods. He writes in the preface, "As an unforeseen bonus for the purposes of this book, evolutionary biology is a historical science forced to use methods different from those of the laboratory sciences. That experience has made the difficulties in devising a scientific approach to human history familiar to me."

Diamond is particularly focused on making complex scientific ideas accessible to the general public. He has authored more than 500 articles and papers—not only numerous scholarly publications, but also articles for mainstream publications such as *Nature*, *Geo*, *Natural History*, and *Discover* (where he serves as a contributing editor). He's also written several trade books for general audiences, most notably *The Third Chimpanzee: The Evolution and Future of the Human Animal* and *Why Is Sex Fun?: The Evolution of Human Sexuality*. His uncanny ability to explain sophisticated concepts to everyday readers has made his books national bestsellers.

The Third Chimpanzee offers a detailed and provocative look at the evolution of humans from our ape ancestors, dwelling especially on the paradox of humanity. We have only a 1.6 percent genetic difference from our chimpanzee relatives, and on a molecular level we're just another species of large mammal. Yet we've come to dominate our planet and develop language, civilizations, religion, art, science—as well as the capacity to destroy ourselves. *The Third Chimpanzee* examines how we got to this point in our evolution, tracing humans from our earliest divergence from chimps. The book is an excellent prequel to *Guns, Germs, and Steel*, as it explains in detail the evolutionary history Diamond briefly summarizes in Chapter 1, "Up to the Starting Line."

Why Is Sex Fun? grew out of the chapters in *The Third Chimpanzee* that addressed human sexuality. In this later book, Diamond offers a genetic, evolutionary explanation for elements of sexuality that are common to humans but make us different from other mammals: why fertility isn't visible in humans, why we have sex in private without always intending to procreate, and why menopause exists, to name a few. In short, *Why Is Sex Fun?* is an entertaining and highly readable account of what drives us sexually.

The academic community has recognized Diamond with impressive awards and titles, both for his work and for his career as a whole. He is a Research Associate in Ornithology at both the American Museum of Natural History and the Los Angeles County Museum of Natural History. He serves on the board of the World Wildlife Fund and has been elected to the National Academy of Sciences, the American Philosophical Society, and the American Academy of Arts and Sciences. He's also received a Burr Award from the National Geographic Society, a Distinguished Achievement Award from the American Gastroenterological Association, and the Bowditch Prize from the American Physiological Society. In 1985, Diamond was awarded the prestigious MacArthur Foundation Genius Grant. In 1999, he was awarded the National Medal of Science, the highest science honor in the United States, for his work in applying Darwin's concepts of evolution to scientific disciplines as various as ecology, conservation biology, physiology, and human history. Perhaps most famously, Diamond won the 1998 Pulitzer Prize for general nonfiction for *Guns, Germs, and Steel.*

Currently, Diamond lives in Los Angeles with his wife, Marie, a clinical psychologist and professor at UCLA, and his twin sons, Max and Joshua. He's in the planning stages of a new book—one that addresses the issue of environmental devastation by examining cultures in history that destroyed their environments and were, in turn, destroyed themselves. In a 1999 interview with the *Boston Globe*, he said, "At the moment the question I find most interesting and important is why in the past did some human societies collapse and others not collapse and what are the practical lessons for our times? That's a big question with big implications: what makes a society fragile?"

The History Hall of Fame

Guns, Germs, and Steel fits solidly into a tradition of books that have tried to craft a comprehensive view of human history.

DIAMOND BREAKS NEW GROUND in many of his assertions in *Guns, Germs, and Steel.* But his isn't the first attempt to explore human history through an interdisciplinary approach and careful use of scientific evidence. Rather, it fits into an existing body of global history that has been gaining considerable ground among historians since the 1990s.

The first efforts at creating a comprehensive view of world history appeared early in the twentieth century. The goal was to expand the study of history from a narrow focus on political events in the West to a detailed study of the histories of all regions of the world and to seek patterns and unifying theories among them.

Examples of this first wave include *The Study of History* (1934–1961), written by historian Arnold Toynbee. This massive twelve-volume set was among the first to examine the histories of every area of the world, looking at the ways in which cultures respond to challenges. Another example is Oswald Spengler's *Decline of the West* (1918–1923), which examines the history of cultures in a search for unifying traits. Spengler concludes that cultures are essentially biological cycles with birth, growth, and inevitable death, and asserts that the West's impending decline is unavoidable. Other well-known scholars who have looked at long-term historical patterns include Patrick Gardiner and Fernand Braudel.

After decades of relative obscurity, the all-encompassing world history reemerged as a trend in the 1970s and has gathered additional momentum in recent years. As before, the goal of this approach is to focus on the big patterns of history and to examine the histories of all areas of the world, not just the Western seats of power. Much of the work historians have done in this field has been to fight "Eurocentrism" in historical inquiry and to examine the effects of colonialism on much of the non-Western world. But these more recent studies also try to integrate relevant knowledge from other disciplines—anthropology, evolutionary science, biogenetics, and others. This mixing has blurred the lines between history and the hard sciences in the quest for universal theories.

Diamond's approach to world history is certainly compatible with these goals. His focus is always on the broadest and most influential trends, and his integration of scientific evidence is compelling. Furthermore, Diamond's perspective—viewing the history of the world through the eyes of often-overlooked cultures like New Guinea's—is unique, even among opponents of Eurocentrism.

Though other historians are far from agreeing on Diamond's conclusions, many of them are engaged in some similar lines of inquiry, and many also center their studies around non-Western cultures. Andre Gunder Frank, author of the widely read *ReOrient: Global Economy in the Asian Age,* suggests that the rise of Western Europe is simply a blip in the long history of an Asia-centered world—a history to which we are now returning. He places the rise of the West in the context of the decline of the East around 1800, suggesting that the West was able to use silver extracted from its colonies to buy into powerful existing world markets in Asia and become economically dominant—at least for a while. (He argues that East Asia is now returning to its place at the center of the world economy.) This theory challenges the long-held belief among Eurocentrics that Europe's rise to dominance was due to unique qualities among its societies, particularly the adoption of capitalism.

Kenneth Pomeranz also examines the competition between East and West, challenging the idea that Europe had a lead before 1800. He argues, among other things, that Europe owes its later dominance to its natural resources, particularly coal and the resources supplied by New World colonies, which allowed for rapid industrialization without ecological sacrifices. Still another scholar, R. Bin Wong, argues that Chinese history has suffered by virtue of the fact that it's been viewed from the perspective of Western history, solely in terms of how it differs from the Western "norm." Wong's book, *China Transformed: Historical Change and the Limits of European Experience*, is a call for a new "Sinocentric" perspective through which historians might gain a more accurate sense of the historical differences between East and West.

Other scholars share with Diamond a desire for a scientific basis for historical inquiry. Among them is Luca Cavalli-Sforza, an expert in the study of human genetics and the role of evolution in world history. His book *The Great Human Diasporas* analyzes the impact of evolution on the movements of peoples throughout history. William H. McNeill's *Plagues and Peoples* also brings a scientific approach to the study of world history. His groundbreaking work, written over twenty years ago and recently reissued, traces the history of infectious diseases throughout all of human history, viewing the major trends of world history through this lens.

Many other historians have also sought to answer Diamond's central question: why and how did Eurasia come to dominate the rest of the world? One recent work that's received a great deal of attention and praise asks the question in economic terms. Harvard University historian David Landes's 1998 bestseller *The Wealth and Poverty of Nations: Why Some are So Rich and Some So Poor*, takes a broad look at the issue and lays out a number of compelling arguments, ranging from climatic differences to societal factors such as openness to new ideas and strength of government. Landes also points to the revolutionary nature of key technologies. In focusing his study on the past 1,000 years of world history, Landes takes Diamond's question further and asks not just why Eurasia dominated the world, but why Europe dominated Asia—and why, by the time of the Industrial Revolution, England dominated Europe.

Diamond is passionate in his opposition to racist explanations for the inequalities among nations and peoples. While racist attitudes may linger among individuals in societies, serious scholars have largely abandoned race-based theories. One notable—and notorious—exception is *The Bell Curve: Intelligence and Class Structure in American Life* by Richard Herrnstein and Charles Murray. This popular book puts forward the controversial argument that there *are* real differences in intelligence among different races and ethnicities. Though Diamond never mentions it directly, it's clear from reading *Guns, Germs, and Steel* that much of his motivation in writing it has been to counter the effects of this type of argument on perceptions of world history and to provide us with compelling alternative explanations.

Required Reading

The controversial *Guns, Germs, and Steel* has quickly worked its way onto reading lists and college syllabi across the country.

PRAISE FOR *GUNS, GERMS, AND STEEL* has been extraordinary, with favorable comments from publications and reviewers across the spectrum. The book has been an enormous commercial and critical success. A national bestseller, it spent two years on *The New York Times* nonfiction list. Even critics who took issue with aspects of the work praised its overall scope and the immense accomplishment it represents. Not surprisingly, *Guns, Germs, and Steel* garnered an armful of awards, including the Phi Beta Kappa Award for Science, the Rhone-Poulenc Prize, the Commonwealth Club of California's Gold Medal, and of course, the Pulitzer Prize for nonfiction. It also appeared as a selection of the Book-of-the-Month Club, the Quality Paperback Book Club, and the History Book Club.

Guns, Germs, and Steel has made a huge impact on college campuses, where it appears on reading lists for courses in many different departments. In the fall of 2001, Cornell University assigned it to every member of the campus community, including incoming freshmen, as part of a program of campus-wide discussions culminating in a guest lecture by Diamond himself.

Reviewers have especially praised Diamond for his willingness to challenge racist explanations of human history. Alfred W. Crosby wrote in the *Los Angeles Times* that Diamond "has done us all a great favor by supplying a rock-solid alternative to the racist answer." Critics have also cheered Diamond for his efforts to apply scientific disciplines to the study of large-scale historical trends. J.R. McNeill of Georgetown University wrote, "[*Guns, Germs, and Steel*] is very persuasive on the usefulness of looking at the very big picture, at broad comparisons and ultimate causes. It is very persuasive on the possibilities of history as a science, and on the value of stepping outside the usual disciplinary boundaries and into the realm of the natural sciences."

James Shreeve of *The New York Times Book Review* called Diamond's work "an ambitious, highly important book" that asked a "powerfully original question." But he also suggested that *Guns, Germs, and Steel* would've benefited from a closer examination of the many disciplines Diamond relied upon—as well as more mention of other specific scholars whose work was critical to his thesis. Shreeve's concern was that Diamond, by simply incorporating the ideas of so many, hinted at an objectivity and unity of perspective that may not have held if he had included more of the conflicting positions within the different disciplines he covers.

Some critics, while admiring much of the book's content, labeled *Guns, Germs, and Steel* "geographic determinism," referring to a methodology that's fallen out of favor among historians. They argued that Diamond perhaps goes too far in attributing everything in history to environment while downplaying the effects of individuals and groups in shaping their own histories. In a somewhat mixed review in *The New York Review of Books*, historian William H. McNeill commented, "No one can doubt the general accuracy of Diamond's account of the environmental differences that he makes so much of. Yet one can doubt whether there was not greater scope for what I would call 'cultural autonomy' than is allowed by Diamond's effort to reduce (or raise?) history to the level of the biological sciences. . . . Diamond's effort to make human history 'scientific' by emphasizing the tyranny of natural environments while neglecting the way diverse symbolic worlds shape and reshape human societies and their physical environments thus seems misguided." McNeill took issue with what he saw as Diamond's tendency to view all of human history as merely the inevitable continuation of environmental trends begun in prehistoric times—thereby minimizing the importance of human actions and cultural innovations.

Diamond replied to this criticism in a letter, in which he summarized the issue like this: "Mr. McNeill faults me for underemphasizing cultural autonomy—i.e., propagated cultural developments independent of environmental differences. Naturally, they are conspicuous in history over shorter times and smaller areas. But, over the hundreds of generations of post-Ice Age human history, and over a large continent's thousands of societies, cultural differences become sifted to approach limits imposed by environmental constraints."

Another criticism of *Guns, Germs, and Steel* was that it neglects the ways in which environments created genetic differences in people as well as plants and animals. These critics claimed that Diamond, in order to discredit arguments of racial superiority, ignored the possibility that the various human races truly are different in a genetic sense. Some argued that the factors of domestication and agriculture may have altered humans themselves, perhaps in considerably different ways across different ethnic groups.

Still other critics took issue with Diamond's strident political correctness and apologetic tone. Some felt his efforts to repudiate racist theories led him to pursue an overly political agenda, casting the failures of have-not societies as inevitable results of their victimhood. David Frum wrote in *Foreign Affairs*, "History has its victims, of course, and Diamond's account of how those victims became victims is powerful and illuminating. But the best way to deal with one's victimhood is by putting it behind one, rather than lounging upon it and indulging it. History should not be written to help: it is scholarship, not social work, and its only criterion of success is truth."

Despite the specific and valid objections of some critics, though, the overall reception of *Guns, Germs, and Steel* and its arguments in mainstream circles was and remains overwhelmingly positive. The book's ability to explain complex ideas while encouraging us to think differently about world history is unprecedented. As *The New Yorker* put it, "The scope and the explanatory power of this book are astounding."

Other Books of Interest

Diamond has followed the lead of other scholars in reexamining human history through the lenses of other disciplines.

○ ○ ○

BY JARED DIAMOND

THE THIRD CHIMPANZEE: THE EVOLUTION AND FUTURE OF THE HUMAN ANIMAL
(HarperCollins, 1992)
Diamond's bestselling account of human evolution. Demonstrates how, despite sharing ninety-eight percent of our genetic material with chimpanzees, we have evolved astonishingly complex features as humans.

WHY IS SEX FUN?: THE EVOLUTION OF HUMAN SEXUALITY
(Basic Books, 1997)
A scientific explanation of the unique features of human sexuality.

BY OTHER AUTHORS

CHINA TRANSFORMED: HISTORICAL CHANGE AND THE LIMITS OF EUROPEAN EXPERIENCE
by R. Bin Wong (Cornell University Press, 1997)
Calls for a new "Sinocentric" perspective on human history.

Guns, Germs, and Steel

THE COLUMBIAN EXCHANGE: BIOLOGICAL CONSEQUENCES OF 1492
by Alfred Crosby (Greenwood, 1972)
A study of the European expansion to the New World, with a focus on the accompanying plants, animals, and germs.

THE ORIGIN OF SPECIES
by Charles Darwin (Gramercy Books, 1998)
The classic, groundbreaking work from the father of evolution, originally published in 1859. Essential for understanding how species adapt to their environments through natural selection.

THE STRUCTURE OF EVOLUTIONARY THEORY
by Stephen Jay Gould (Harvard University Press, 2002)
A complete history and analysis of classical and twentieth-century evolutionary theory from one of America's best-known scientists.

REORIENT: GLOBAL ECONOMY IN THE ASIAN AGE
by Andre Gunder Frank (University of California Press, 1998)
Argues that Western dominance is merely a blip in the Asian-centered history of the world.

THE BELL CURVE: INTELLIGENCE AND CLASS STRUCTURE IN AMERICAN LIFE
by Richard Herrnstein and Charles Murray (Free Press, 1994)
An attempt to cast differences in intelligence in racial terms. A rather notorious book that some critics considered racist propaganda, it definitely provides a different viewpoint from Guns, Germs, and Steel.

THE EUROPEAN MIRACLE: ENVIRONMENTS, ECONOMIES AND GEOPOLITICS IN THE HISTORY OF EUROPE AND ASIA
by E.L. Jones (Cambridge University Press, 1987)
Examines the differences among the histories of China, India, Islam, and Europe.

THE DAWN OF HUMAN CULTURE
by Richard G. Klein and Blake Edgar (John Wiley & Sons, 2002)
An anthropological look at the history of human development, and more specifically, the human brain.

THE WEALTH AND POVERTY OF NATIONS: WHY SOME ARE SO RICH AND SOME SO POOR
by David S. Landes (W.W. Norton & Co., 1998)
A bestseller that analyzes the past millennium of history and asks the question, "Why Europe?"

PLAGUES AND PEOPLES
by William McNeill (Doubleday, 1976)
Extremely influential, credited with getting historians to recognize the impact of disease on world history.

THE LEVER OF RICHES
by Joel Mokyr (Oxford University Press, 1990)
Examines the history of technology, focusing on the question of why the rate of development of technology has varied at different times in different places.

THE RISE OF THE WESTERN WORLD: A NEW ECONOMIC HISTORY
by Douglass C. North and Robert Paul Thomas (Cambridge University Press, 1973)
An argument that the success of the Western world has stemmed from its legal and political institutions.

THE GREAT DIVERGENCE: CHINA, EUROPE AND THE MAKING OF THE MODERN WORLD ECONOMY
by Kenneth Pomeranz (Princeton University Press, 2000)
Argues that Europe and Asia were on equal footing as late as 1800 and that Europe's rise was due to the availability of coal and the resources supplied by New World colonies.

THE ORIGINS OF AGRICULTURE: AN EVOLUTIONARY PERSPECTIVE
by David Rindos (Academic Press, 1984)
A Darwinian approach to the archaeological record of early humans.

HOW THE WEST GREW RICH: THE ECONOMIC TRANSFORMATION OF THE INDUSTRIAL WORLD
by Nathan Rosenberg and L.E. Birdzell Jr. (Basic Books, 1986)
An exploration of the rise of capitalism and the impact of technology.

CONQUESTS AND CULTURES: AN INTERNATIONAL HISTORY
by Thomas Sowell (Basic Books, 1999)

Examines the ways in which military conquest both destroys and spreads culture.

NONZERO: THE LOGIC OF HUMAN DESTINY
by Robert Wright (W.W. Norton, 2000)

An exploration of human social evolution within the framework of modern game theory. Argues that human culture becomes increasingly complex as a result of continuous, self-feeding nonzero-sum relationships.

DOMESTICATION OF PLANTS IN THE OLD WORLD
by Daniel Zohary and Maria Hopf (Oxford University Press, 1993)

A detailed account of plant domestication in Western Eurasia. Provides archaeological and genetic evidence about the domestication and spread of each significant crop.